PEP HIGH FIVE

Pre-school Illustrated Chinese for Kids

LEVEL ONE　BOOK 3

哈哈镜　Magic Mirror

Jennifer Sun　Alex Shirran　Bai Lian

人民教育出版社
PEOPLE'S EDUCATION PRESS

图书在版编目（CIP）数据

哈哈镜／（加）孙宏，（加）希拉（Shirran, A.）
白莲编．—北京：人民教育出版社，2008
（PEP High Five幼儿图画汉语．第1级．第3册）
ISBN 978－7－107－21280－2

Ⅰ．哈…
Ⅱ．①孙…②希…③白…
Ⅲ．汉语—对外汉语教学—教材
Ⅳ．H195.4

中国版本图书馆CIP数据核字（2008）第179001号

人民教育出版社出版发行
网址：http:// www.pep.com.cn
北京盛通印刷股份有限公司印装　全国新华书店经销
2008年8月第1版　2009年12月第2次印刷
开本：890毫米×1 240毫米　1/20　印张：1.6　插页：1

ISBN 978-7-107-21280-2　定价：15.00元
G · 14390

nǐ hǎo wǒ shì dòu dou

你好，我是豆豆。

Hello, I am Bean.

bí zi

鼻子

nose

Where are their noses?

yǎn jing

眼睛

eye

Where are their eyes?

ěr duo

耳朵 ear

Where are their ears?

zuǐ

嘴

mouth

Where are their mouths?

tóu fa
头发 hair

Where are their hairs?

jiǎo
脚
foot

Where are their feet?

shǒu

手

hand

Where are their hands?

tuǐ

腿 leg

Where are their legs?

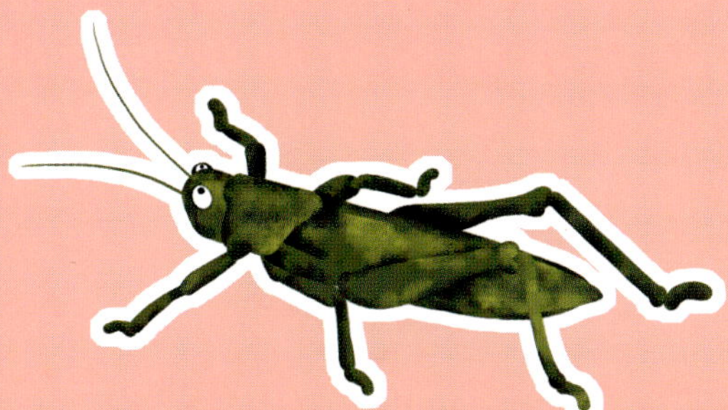

yá chǐ

牙齿 tooth

Where are their teeth?

gē bo

胳膊 arm

Where are their arms?

Certificate

Congratulations! You have successfully completed the PEP Pre-school Chinese.

Level One Book 3

bí zi
鼻子

yǎn jing
眼睛

ěr duo
耳朵

tóu fa
头发

zuǐ
嘴

shǒu
手

jiǎo
脚

tuǐ
腿

yá chǐ
牙齿

gē bo
胳膊

LET'S DO!

1 *Put your hand on this page and draw around the edge. Then color the Chinese character "手" in the middle.*

手

LET'S DO!

2 *Put your foot on this page and draw around the edge. Then color the Chinese character "脚" in the middle.*

3 *Draw the missing body parts according to the Chinese characters.*

bí zi
鼻子

yǎn jing
眼睛

zuǐ
嘴

ěr duo
耳朵

LET'S DO!

4 *Place the stickers in the correct location.*

5 *Circle the correct Chinese characters according to the pictures.*

tuǐ
腿

shǒu
手

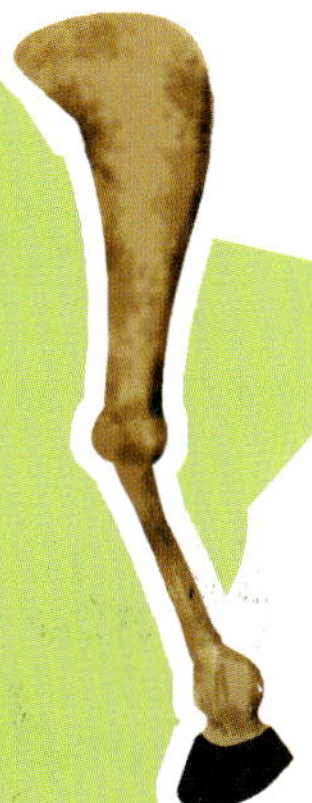

tóu fa
头发

bí zi
鼻子

gē bo
胳膊

jiǎo
脚

zuǐ
嘴

yá chǐ
牙齿

LET'S DO!

6 *Play this game with your dad and mom.*

后记

《PEP High Five幼儿图画汉语》是人民教育出版社与中国、加拿大两国汉语和学前教育专家合作的结晶，根据“以结果为基础”的教育理念设计。这套汉英双语系列丛书供2岁～6岁以英语为母语的幼儿汉语学习者使用，也可供国内幼儿学习英语使用。

本丛书共四级，每级四册，主要特点是：

- 明确幼儿汉语学习者每级应该达到的阅读、行为和社会交往目标；
- 阅读材料具有很强的趣味性和参与性；
- 评估手段和学习活动的操作简单明了；
- 练习及活动互动有趣；
- 内容灵活，适合学习者根据自身的语言能力和进度进行学习；
- 插图精美，富有启发性，有助于促进学习者对内容的理解。

本丛书的作者是Jennifer Sun女士（加拿大）、Alex Shirran先生（加拿大）和白莲博士（中国）。责任编辑常志丹。审稿王世友、郑旺全。插图绘制金葆工作室。邢恩沐（Kevin）小朋友提供部分插图创意。

人民教育出版社汉语国际推广中心

2008年5月

POSTSCRIPT

The *PEP High Five Pre-school Illustrated Chinese for Kids* is a product created collaboratively by the People's Education Press (PEP), Chinese language experts, and pre-school educators in Canada and China. Being structured according to the Outcome-based Education (OBE) theory, it is a series of bilingual books that targets pre-school Chinese language learners aged 2 to 6 and whose native language is English. It may also be used by children in China who are learning English as a second language.

This series includes four levels and each level includes four books. It has many positive features that enhance learning. Some of these features are:

- Clearly stated reading, behavioral, and social objectives that students are expected to reach at each reading stage;
- Exciting and engaging reading material that covers all of the learning objectives;
- Easy-to-use assessment standards and activities;
- Interactive and fun student worksheets and activities;
- Content that allows students to work at their own pace and according to their own individual language ability;
- Colorful and inspiring artwork that aids in the students' reading comprehension.

The authors of the series are Ms. Jennifer Sun (Canada), Mr. Alex Shirran (Canada) and Dr. Bai Lian (China). The editor of this series is Mr. Chang Zhidan. Reviewers are Mr. Wang Shiyou and Mr. Zheng Wangquan. Illustrations are by Jin Bao Art Workshop. Some ideas of the illustrations are provided by nine-year-old Kevin, Enmu Xing.

The PEP International Center for Chinese Language and Culture
May, 2008